DISTRIBUTED ENERGY SYSTEMS

DISTRIBUTED ENERGY SYSTEMS

SHIN'YA OBARA

Nova Science Publishers, Inc.
New York

For permission to use material from this book please contact us:
Telephone 631-231-7269; Fax 631-231-8175
Web Site: http://www.novapublishers.com

NOTICE TO THE READER

LIBRARY OF CONGRESS CATALOGING-IN-PUBLICATION DATA

ISBN: 978-1-60692-543-0

Available upon request

Published by Nova Science Publishers, Inc. ⏎ New York

CONTENTS

Chapter 1

OPERATION PLAN OF A COMBINED FUEL CELL COGENERATION USING GENETIC ALGORITHM

INTRODUCTION

From deregulation of energy business, and an environmental problem, the installation spread of the small-scale distribution power due to a fuel cell and a heat engine is expected. Under the objective function set up by the designer or the user, optimization planning that controls small-scale distribution power is required. In dynamic operation planning of the energy plant, the analysis method using mixed integer linear programming is developed [1, 2]. For the compound energy systems of solar modules and fuel cell cogeneration, there have been no reports of the optimization of operation planning. Therefore, there are no results showing the relationship between the objective function given to the combined system and operation planning. Such as a solar modules or wind power, green-energy equipment is accompanied by the fluctuation of an output in many cases. Almost all green energy equipment requires backup by commercial power, fuel cells, heat engines, etc. Operation planning of the system that utilizes renewable energy differs by the objective function and power and heat load pattern. Thus, this chapter investigates the operation planning of the compound energy system composed of proton exchange membrane fuel cell cogeneration with methanol steam-reforming equipment, a solar module, geo-thermal heat pump, heat storage, water electrolysis equipment, commercial power, and a kerosene boiler. In such a complex energy system, facility cost is expensive. However, in this chapter, it investigates as a case of the independent power source for backlands with renewable energy. This chapter considers the operation planning of a system, and the optimization of equipment capacity. The Genetic Algorithm (hereafter described as GA) applicable to a nonlinear problem with many variables is installed into the optimization calculation of the operation planning of the system [3]. In the operation analysis of a complex energy system, Mixed Integer Programming (MIP) other than GA can be used. Because the nonlinear analysis using MIP is made to approximate using a linear expression of relations, it is considered that an error is large. On the other hand, GA is applicable to the analysis of the nonlinear problem of many variables. The range of the analysis accuracy obtained by calculation with GA is understood that it can use industrially. In GA, the design variable of energy equipment is shown with many gene models. In this chapter, the objective functions given to the system were set up as (1) Minimization of error in demand-and-supply balance, (2) Minimization of the operation cost (fuel consumption) of energy equipment, (3) Minimization of the carbon dioxide gas emission accompanying operation, and (4) Minimization of the three objective functions described above. The load pattern in winter (February) and summer (August) of the average individual house in Sapporo, Japan, is used for the energy demand model shown with a case study [4]. This chapter described the operation plan of the independence energy system when installing a methanol steam-reforming type fuel cell and renewable energy into a cold region house. Such complex operation optimization of the energy system did not have a report until now. Consequently, the method of installing and analyzing the GA apply to the nonlinear problem of many variables was proposed. In points of equipment cost, it is difficult for a proposed system to spread generally. However, the installation to the area where the commercial power is not fixed is possible.

FUEL CELL, SOLAR MODULES, AND GEO-THERMAL HEAT PUMP COMBINED SYSTEM

Scheme of Combined System

Figure 1 shows the energy system scheme examined in this chapter. A combined system consists of a solar module (18), PEMFC-CGS (PEMFC: proton exchange membrane, fuel cell CGS: co-generation, the fuel cell is (1), the reforming equipment is (2)-(5) and (12), geo-thermal heat pump, (17), boiler, (8), commercial electric power, heat storage tank (10), and the water electrolysis equipment is (13)-(15)). Water electrolysis equipment is used to store electrical power with hydrogen and oxygen. The arrowhead in this figure shows the substance or direction of energy flux. Each system of solar module, commercial electrical power, and PEMFC-CGS is changed with a changeover switch (6), and electrical power is supplied to the consumer. However, electrical power is not at once supplied to the demand side from two or more power systems.

An electric heater (9) is installed inside the heat storage tank, and electric power is changed into heat and can be stored. Hydrogen and oxygen can be produced if electric power is supplied to an electrolysis tank (13). Hydrogen and oxygen are stored in tanks (14) and (15), respectively, and these are supplied to PEMFC and can be generated at an arbitrary time. When the heat produced by the geo-thermal heat pump exceeds the quantity demanded, surplus heat is stored in the heat storage tank. Although the exhaust heat of PEMFC and the methanol steam-reforming equipment is also supplied to the heat storage tank, when the total amount of heat exceeds the heat storage capacity, heat is radiated with a radiator (7). Tap water has heat exchanged for the heat transfer medium inside the heat storage tank, and moreover controls the temperature of this tap water by the boiler, and supplies hot water to the consumer.

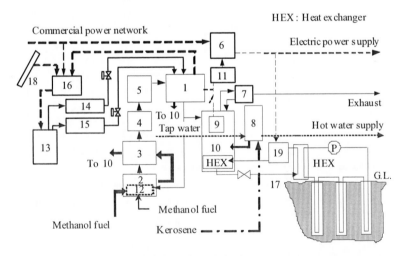

1. Fuel cell stack, 2. Vaporizer, 3. Reformer, 4. Shifter, 5. CO oxidation, 6. Change over switch, 7. Radiator, 8. Back-up boiler, 9. Electric heater, 10. Heat Storage tank, 11. DC/AC converter, 12. Catalytic combustor, 13. Electrolysis tank, 14. H_2 tank, 15. O_2 tank, 16. Changeover switch, 17. Geothermal heat pump system, 18. Solar modules, 19. Compressor

Figure 1. PEMFC-CGS, Heat-pump and solar module combined system for houses.

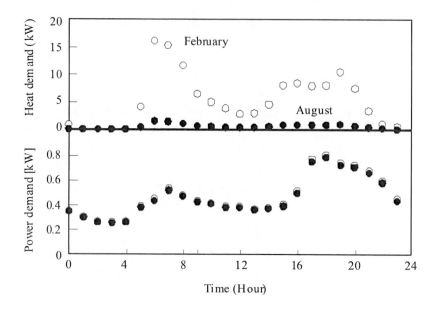

Figure 2. Energy demand of Sapporo-city (Narita *et al*, 1996).

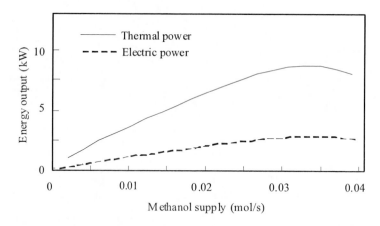

Figure 3. Characteristics of fuel cell stack with methanol steam reforming (Obara *et al.,* 2003).

Methanol fuel is supplied to the reformed gas system of the methanol steam-reforming equipment, and the catalytic-combustion equipment (12) installed in the evaporator (2). Kerosene fuel is supplied to the boiler (8). The energy demand pattern used for analysis is a model in February (winter) and August (summer) in the average individual house in Sapporo in Japan, and shows this in Figure 2. For

Sapporo, a cold, snowy area, the annual average temperature is 288 K, and the mean temperature in February and August is 269 K and 294 K, respectively. The operating period of a system is made into 23:00 from 0:00 of a representation day, and sampling time is expressed by t_k $(k = 0, 1, 2, ..., 23)$. The initial values of the capacity of each energy device set up the value used for the usual individual house. The specifications of each energy device are shown in Table 1.

Table 1. Energy device specifications

Solar module	
Area	6.0 m^2
Electric energy output	3kW (Maximum)
Fuel cell	
Type	Proton-exchange membrane fuel cell
Fuel	Water/Methanol=1.4/1.0 (mole ratio)
Reforming type	Methanol steam reforming
Electric energy output	Maximum 3kW
Thermal energy output	9kW (Maximum)
Commercial power	5kW (Maximum)
Heat pump	
Type	Geothermal heat source
Energy source	Electricity
p-h diagram	See Fig.4
Thermal energy output	5kW (Maximum)
COP	3.0
Electrolysis device [8]	
Electrolysis efficient	0.85 (Constant)
Accumulation of electricity	180MJ
Backed boiler	
Fuel	Kerosene
Efficincy	0.85 (Constant)
Thermal energy output	40kW (Maximum)
Thermal storage tank	
Thermal storage capacity	180MJ
Heat medium temperature	353K (Maximum)
Thermal storage efficiency	0.95

Compared with the condition of the steady operation of the methanol reformer, the characteristics of a startup and a shutdown differ greatly. Cold start operation and shutdown operation require about 20 minutes, respectively. In the analysis of this section, it is assumed that the startup of the methanol reformer is always a hot start.

Relational Expression

(1) Energy Output of PEMFC-CGS

3kW methanol steam reforming type PEMFC shown in Figure 3 is used for the output characteristic of the fuel cell introduced into analysis [5]. The horizontal axis of Figure 3 is divided into two or more zones, and the output characteristics are given by the analysis program by using the secondary least-squares method approximation for each range. The electric power output at the time of supplying and generating hydrogen and oxygen stored by water electrolysis to a fuel cell is expressed by Equation (1).

$$E_{FS,tk} = I_{c,tk} \cdot E_{V,tk} - \Delta W_{FS,tk} = \frac{Q_{f,tk} \cdot F_d}{E_c} \cdot E_{V,tk} - \Delta W_{FS,tk} \tag{1}$$

Here, $I_{c,tk}$, $E_{V,tk}$, $\Delta W_{FS,tk}$, $Q_{f,tk}$, F_d and E_c express current, voltage, power loss of a cell stack, hydrogen amount of supply, Faraday constant and chemical equivalent, respectively.

(2) Heat Output of Geo-thermal Heat Pump

Figure 4 is a *p-h* diagram of Refrigerant HC-12a [6], used by the geo-thermal heat pump [7, 8]. This refrigerant is a mixed refrigerant of propane, butane, and isobutene. Although the output characteristics of the heat pump were the analysis of soil temperature T_L and condensation temperature T_H exactly, coefficient of performance COP_{tk} was set to 3.0 in this section.

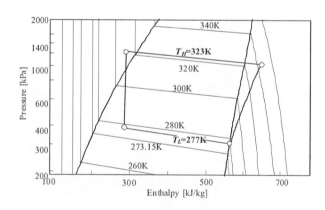

Figure 4. p-h diagram of Refrigerant AHC-12a (HC-TECH Inc., 1997).

(3) Characteristic Equation of Water Electrolysis Tank

From sampling time t_k to Δt, the electric power supplied to an electrolysis tank is expressed by E_{EL,t_k}, and the efficiency of the electrolysis tank is expressed by ϕ_{EL}. In this case, hydrogen quantity Q_{H2,t_k} to be produced is calculated by Equation (2). Moreover, the amount of production of oxygen is similarly calculated. The efficiency of water electrolyzer refers to the results of a study [9] that used the proton exchange membrane, and ϕ_{EL} is set as 0.85.

$$Q_{H2,t_k} = \frac{E_{EL,t_k} \cdot E_c}{F_d \cdot E_V} \cdot \phi_{EL} \tag{2}$$

In calculations for this case study, the hydrogen and oxygen are pressurized to 1.0 MPa, respectively. The work of the compressor is assumed to be compression work for an ideal gas. The whole compressor efficiency including an inverter controller loss and the power consumption in an electric motor, transfer loss of power, loss with insufficient air leak and cooling, and other machine losses is set up to 50%.

(4) Characteristic Equation of Heat Storage Tank and Boiler

The conditional expression showing heat storage characteristics is given by Equation (3) and Equation (4) using the amount of maximum heat storage $S_{St,\max}$, and maximum temperature $T_{St,\max}$ of the heat medium. The capacity and the specific heat of the heat storage medium are expressed by V and C_p, and outside air temperature is expressed by T_∞ (The heat medium is assumed to be calcium chloride). Moreover, the heat storage temperature at time t_k is calculated by $T_{St,t_k} = S_{St,t_k} / (\rho \cdot C_p \cdot V)$. Here, ρ express density of heat storage medium.

$$0 \leq S_{St,t_k} \leq S_{St,\max} \tag{3}$$

$$T_{\infty,t_k} \leq T_{St,t_k} \leq T_{St,\max} \tag{4}$$

The characteristic equation of heat storage tank between time t_k and Δt is given by Equation (5).

$$S_{St,t_k} - S_{St,t_{k-1}} = \left\{ H_{St,in,t_k} - H_{St,out,t_k} - \phi_{St} \cdot \rho \cdot C_p \cdot V \cdot (T_{St,t_k} - T_{\infty,t_k}) \right\} \cdot \Delta t \tag{5}$$

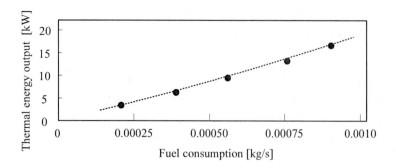

Figure 5. Thermal energy output of boiler.

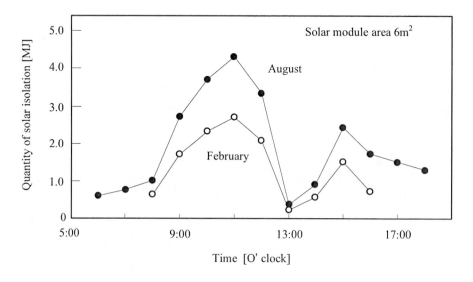

Figure 6. Time change of solar module output (Nagano et al., 2002).

H_{St,in,t_k} and H_{St,out,t_k} express the heat input and heat output of the heat storage tank, respectively. The third term in the right-hand bracket of Equation (5) includes outside air temperature T_{∞,t_k} supposing heat storage loss is dependent on outside air temperature. However, in the analysis in this section, the efficiency of heat storage ϕ_{St} is set to 0.95, and change in outside air temperature is not taken into consideration. Figure 5 shows the relationship between the fuel consumption of a boiler and hot-water-supply output. It is expressed with the calorific value of the fuel being α_{Boiler}, the boiler efficiency being ϕ_{Boiler}, and the fuel-supply quantity of flow being $F_{Boiler,tk}$, and the characteristic equation of a boiler is given by the following equation.

$$H_{Boiler,tk} = \alpha_{Boiler} \cdot F_{Boiler,tk} \cdot \phi_{Boiler} \tag{6}$$

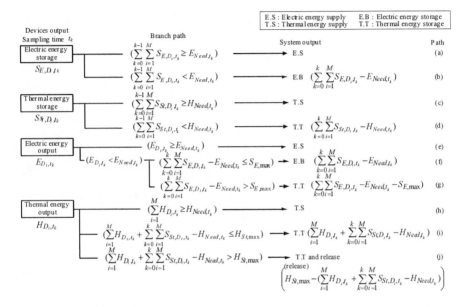

Figure 7. Energy supply path.

(5) Characteristic Equation of Solar Module

Figure 6 shows the results of measurement of the production of electricity of the solar module in February and August in Sapporo [10]. However, the panel was vertically installed so that this solar module would not be covered in snow in winter. Therefore, the production of electricity decreases as shown in the results of Figure 6 at 13:00.

Energy Supply Path

The energy equipment is expressed by D_i , and let subscript i ($i = 1, 2, 3, ..., M$, M are the number of pieces of equipment) be the equipment number. The electric power and heat that are outputted by energy device D_i

follow one path (a) to (j) as shown in Figure 7. When electric energy $E_{Di,tk}$ generated by the system exceeds power demand $E_{Need,tk}$, hydrogen and oxygen are produced and stored by water electrolysis. Moreover, it is also possible to change electric power into heat with a heater, to shift time, and to supply the demand side.

ENERGY BALANCE AND OBJECTIVE FUNCTION

Objective Function of System

The objective function given to the system is given by (1) Minimization of error in demand-and-supply balance, (2) Minimization of the operation cost (fuel consumption) of the energy equipment, (3) Minimization of the carbon dioxide gas emission accompanying operation, and (4) Minimization of the three objective functions described above. Equation (7) and Equation (8) are energy balance equations of electric power and heat, respectively.

$$E_{FS,tk} + E_{Utility,tk} + E_{Stp,tk} = E_{System,tk} + \Delta E_{EL,tk} + \Delta E_{HP,tk} + \Delta E_{CPH,tk} + \Delta E_{CPO,tk} + E_{H,tk} \tag{7}$$

$$\alpha_{FS} \cdot F_{FS,tk} \cdot \phi_{FS} + \alpha_{Boiler} \cdot F_{Boiler,tk} \cdot \phi_{Boiler} + H_{HP,tk} + H_{St,tk} = H_{System,tk} + H_{Rad,tk} + \Delta H_{St,tk} \tag{8}$$

The left-hand side in Equation (7) and Equation (8) is the amount of energy inputted into the system, and the right-hand side expresses the amount of energy outputted from the system. Here, $E_{FS,tk}$, $E_{Utility,tk}$, $E_{Stp,tk}$ and $E_{System,tk}$ express electric power of fuel cell stack, commercial power and power storage, respectively. $\Delta E_{EL,tk}$, $\Delta E_{HP,tk}$, $\Delta E_{CPH,tk}$, $\Delta E_{CPO,tk}$ and $E_{H,tk}$ express power consumption of electrolyzer, heat pump, hydrogen compressor, oxygen compressor and heater, respectively. α_{FS} and α_{Boiler} express calorific value of fuel of fuel cell stack and boiler. ϕ_{FS} and ϕ_{Boiler} express efficiency of fuel cell stack and boiler. $F_{FS,tk}$ and $F_{Boiler,tk}$ express fuel quantity of flow of fuel cell stack and boiler. $H_{HP,tk}$, $H_{St,tk}$, $H_{System,tk}$, $H_{Rad,tk}$ and $\Delta H_{St,tk}$ express heat of heat pump, heat storage tank, system, radiator and heat storage loss, respectively.

Objective function (1) described in Introduction is an operating pattern when the difference in input-output of energy balance Equation (7) and Equation (8) serves as the minimum. Objective function (2) is an operating pattern when fuel cost and commercial power cost serve as the minimum. The operation cost of equipment D_i between time t_k and Δt is calculated from fuel flow rate F_{D_i,t_k} and unit fuel price C_{fuel,D_i} that are supplied to the equipment. Therefore, the operation cost of the whole system is calculated by Equation (9). Here, $C_{Utility,t_k}$ express commercial power cost.

$$C_{System,t_k} = \sum_{i=1}^{M} \left(C_{fuel,D_i} \cdot F_{D_i,t_k} \cdot \Delta t \right) + C_{Utility,t_k} \tag{9}$$

Objective function (3) expresses the operation pattern whose amount of greenhouse gas discharge calculated from the fuel consumption is the minimum. Amount of emission W_{System,t_k} of greenhouse gases is calculated by Equation (10). However, the number of gas compositions that contribute to greenhouse gas discharged by equipment D_i is expressed by S.

$$W_{System,t_k} = \sum_{i=1}^{M} \sum_{j=1}^{S} \left(G_{D_i,EX_j} \cdot \varepsilon_{D_i,EX_j,t_k} \cdot F_{D_i,t_k} \cdot \Delta t \right) \tag{10}$$

Table 2. Energy cost and greenhouse-warming coefficient (Japanese Environment Agency, 2000)

Kerosene fuel	0.01097 Dollar/J
	3.099 kg？CO_2/kg
	2.026 kg/Dollar
Methanol fuel	0.01772 Dollar/J
	1.379 kg？CO_2/kg
Commercial power	0.0647 Dollar/J (9:00-21:00)
	0.01515 Dollar/J (22:00-8:00)
	0.000099167 kg？CO_2/kJ

Table 3. Calculation result of each purposes of February (Kerosene (kg))

Minimization of	operation cost	the error of demand-and -supply balance	greenhouse gas
Minimization of operation cost	**14.72** (15.36)	0.439	13.76 (13.35)
Minimization of the error of demand-and-supply balance	22.40	**0.0170**	18.82
Minimization of the amount of green-house gas discharge	15.66	0.426	**13.16**

Table 4. Calculation result of each purposes of August (Kerosene (kg))

	operation cost	the error of demand-and -supply balance	greenhouse gas discharge
Minimization of operation cost	**3.61** (4.28)	0.795	3.42 (2.60)
Minimization of the error of demand-and -supply balance	6.85	**0.0247**	4.174
Minimization of the amount of green-house gas discharge	5.27	0.199	**2.55**

Here, G_{D_i,EX_j} expresses a global-warming factor per unit weight of fuel, $\varepsilon_{D_i,EX_j,t_k}$ being the weight concentration of EX_j, and F_{D_i,t_k} being the amount of fuel supply to equipment D_i. Table 2 shows fuel cost and a global-warming factor [11], and is analyzed using these values in an analysis case.

Multi-objective Optimization

As shown in Equation (11), the operation pattern that minimizes the sum that multiplies each objective function by weight is a multiple-objective optimal solution.

$$\text{minimize} \left(\sum_{t_k=1}^{Period} \sum_{j=1}^{N_p} w_j \cdot f_j(x_{t_k}) \right) \tag{11}$$

In order for the same level to compare the amount of energy loss, operation cost, and amount of greenhouse gas emission, each value was replaced to the amount of kerosene and evaluated. w_j in Equation (11) is given beforehand and the value of this equation searches for the minimum solution using GA. Here, w_j , $f_j(x_{t_k})$ and N_p express weight of an objective function, objective function and number of objective functions, respectively.

ANALYSIS RESULTS

Results of Optimization

Tables 3 and 4 are the calculation results when optimizing under each objective function using the energy demand pattern of a representative day in February and August, and are converting all values into a kerosene weight. The number in ( ) of the table is the value of the conventional energy system (using commercial power and a kerosene boiler). If this system is optimized by operation cost minimization, compared with the cost of the conventional system, there will be a maximum of 4% and 16% reduction in February and August, respectively. Reduction rates differ every month because the energy demanded and the solar module output are different.

Equipment Capacity

The analysis results of the ratio of maximum output to equipment capacity at the time of planning operation with each objective function (this value is described as RMC below) are shown in Table 5 and Table 6. If the value of RMC is lower than 1, a decrease in the initialized equipment capacity (Table 1) is possible. On the other hand, equipment with a larger value of RMC than 1 has insufficient capacity. The analysis results of RMC of heat storage and power storage (storage of hydrogen and oxygen by water electrolysis) when operating the system under each objective function are shown in Figure 8. From the results of Figure 8, the capacity reduction ratio of a heat storage tank and power storage equipment can be seen. From the method described above, the optimization of the capacity of each piece of equipment that composes a system can be designed.

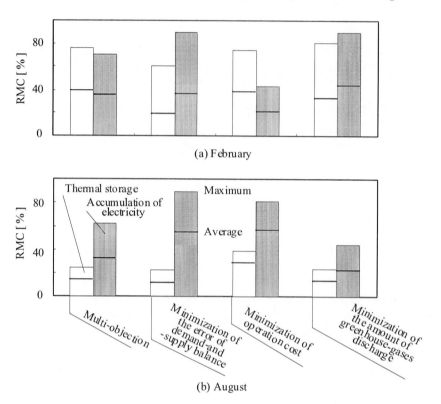

Figure 8. Energy storage result.

Objective Function and Characteristics of Operation Plan

Figures 9 and 10 show the balance results of electric power and heat when optimizing an operation plan under each objective function using the energy demand pattern of representative February and August days. "System energy output" in these figures is the characteristic of electric power and heat outputted by the system configuration equipment. However, power storage output and heat storage output are not included in this characteristic, but are separately shown as "Storage". Moreover, the energy demanded is shown as "Demand".

In Figure 9 and Figure 10, although the characteristic of "Demand" is flat, there ate times when the characteristic of "System energy output" is extremely large. The reason for this is that it stores energy for a short period in the system, when the stored energy is released in large quantities. Figure 11 shows the ratio of energy outputted by each piece of equipment. The operation plan when optimizing the energy system of Figure 1 under different objective functions from the analysis results described above has the characteristics described below.

Table 5. RMC of February (RMC=Maximum output/Cevice capacity)

	Commercial power	Fuel cell	Solar module		Heat pump	Boiler
			Electricity use	Heat use		
Minimization of the error of demand-and-supply balance	0.90	0.906	0.338	0.662	0.980	0.964
Operation cost minimization	0.57	0	0.361	0.639	0.982	0.990
Greenhouse gas minimization	0.82	0.899	0.207	0.793	1.00	1.00

Table 6. RMC of August

	Commercial power	Fuel cell	Solar module		Heat pump	Boiler
			Electricity use	Heat use		
	0.87	0.714	0.159	0.841	0.604	0.255
Operation cost minimization	0.81	0.631	0.566	0.434	0.614	0.564
Greenhouse gas minimization	0.48	0.503	0.444	0.556	0.890	0.139

(1) Operation Plan of the Minimization of Error in Demand-and-Supply Balance

As Figure 9 (a) and Figure 10 (a) show, the stored electric power and heat is mostly used up at 23:00. Moreover, as shown in Table 5 and Table 6, both months are high-output months, and the operating point of a fuel cell is planned so that partial-load operation is avoided. The operation of a fuel cell with a high value of RMC (Maximum output / Cevice capacity) avoids low-efficiency, partial-load operation.

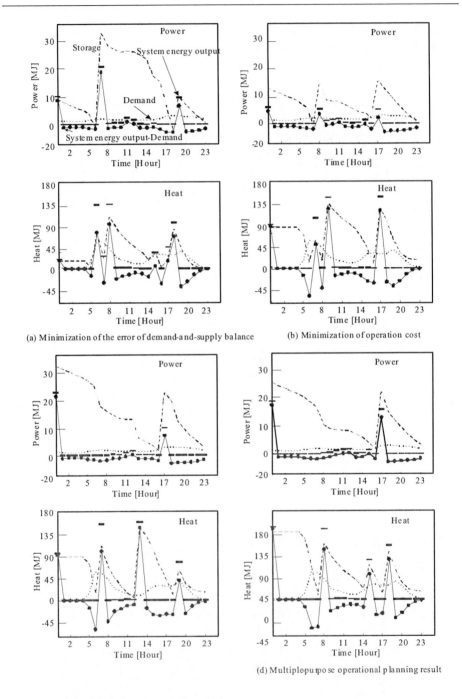

(a) Minimization of the error of demand-and-supply balance

(b) Minimization of operation cost

(d) Multiple-purpose operational planning result

Figure 9. Operational planning result of February.

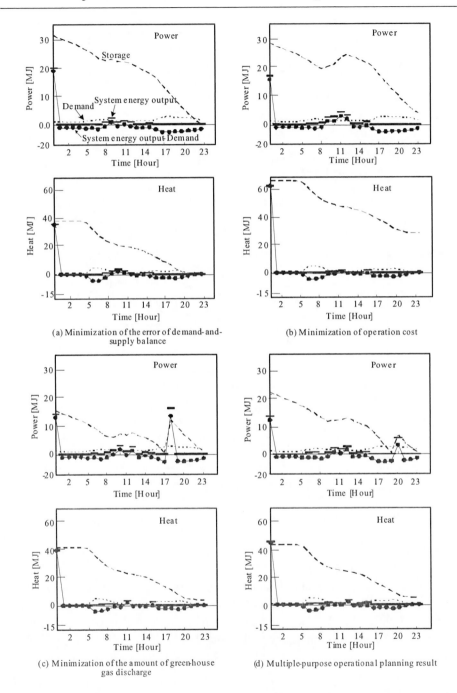

(a) Minimization of the error of demand-and-supply balance

(b) Minimization of operation cost

(c) Minimization of the amount of green-house gas discharge

(d) Multiple-purpose operational planning result

Figure 10. Operational planning result of August.

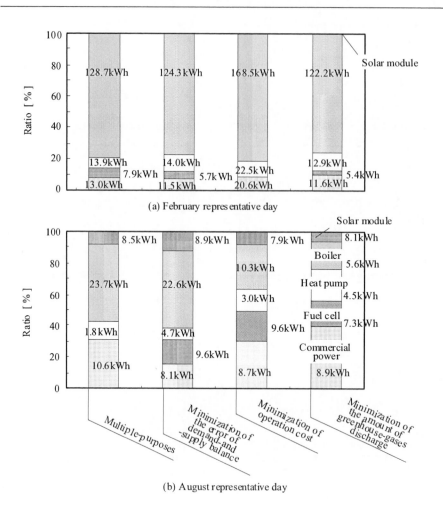

Figure 11. Result of Energy output component.

(2) Operation Plan of the Minimization of Equipment Operation Cost (Fuel Consumption)

From the results of Table 5 and Table 6, the electric power generated by the solar module is supplied to the demand side with electric power rather than heat compared with other objective functions. This is because the cost of this method of producing is high compared with the amount of heat. As the results of Table 5 show, the output of commercial power lowers and there is no fuel cell operation. In optimization with this objective function, operation that suspends operation, converts power into heat, stores power is planned.

(3) Operation Plan of the Minimization of the Greenhouse Gas Emission

From the results of Table 5, operation of a heat pump and boiler is planned with a maximum-output point on representative February days with great heat demand. Moreover, application is planned with a value with a high supply rate by the heat of the solar module, and high RMC of the fuel cell. On the other hand, heat supply, rather than the boiler, is mainly concerned with the heat pump according to the results of representative August days with little heat demanded as shown in Table 6 and Figure 11 (b).

(4) Operation Plan of the Minimization of Multi-Objective Functions

When operating the system under a multi-objective function, the result of Figure 8 to RMC is a value near the average value adding each objective function. As shown in Figure 9 (d) and Figure 10 (d), the operation plan under this objective function includes the characteristic of the operation plan of other objective functions.

CONCLUSIONS

How the operation optimization of the combined system of PEMFC-CGS, a solar module, a geo-thermal heat pump, heat storage and power storage equipment, a commercial electric power, and a boiler using GA should be analyzed was described. The capacity optimization of equipment that composes a system was considered from the analysis results. If the capacity of each energy device changes with the objective functions given to the system and examination of equipment cost is added to the results in this section, it can be utilized in real design. Moreover, the characteristics when planning the operation of a system under each objective function were investigated. As a result, for example, the minimization objective of operation cost, operation that suspends operation and converts power into heat, power storage operation is planned. If the objective function concerning minimization of greenhouse gas discharge is given to the system, there will be many opportunities to use the electric power of a solar module as heat; moreover, heat supply mainly concerned with the heat pump rather than the boiler is planned. In the design and operation plan of a combined system containing renewable energy equipment, care should be taken concerning the composition and operating method that change greatly according to objectives given to the system.

Chapter 2

ROUTE PLANNING OF HEAT SUPPLY PIPING IN A FUEL CELL ENERGY NETWORK

INTRODUCTION

Small-scale fuel cells are distributed in houses, apartment houses, small-scale stores, etc, and power and heat are supplied to them. High facility cost, efficiency fall at the time of partial load, and mismatch of heat output to power generation are issues of this technology. Therefore, in this section, a technology where power and heat demand of tens of or buildings or less correspond by the centralization system and by the distributed system of fuel cells is investigated. The fuel cell centralization system supplies energy to each building from a fuel cell and auxiliary machinery that have been prepared in one arbitrarily selected building. On the other hand, the fuel cell distribution system supplies energy by placing a fuel cell in each building. Until now, improvement in efficiency with cooperation system control [12], peak cut of the power load using a water electrolyzer [13], and estimation of the amount of heat radiation of the hot-water piping for exhaust heat supply [14] are discussed regarding the fuel cell distribution system. When supplying energy using the central system, a heat energy system (hot-water piping) and a power system (power transmission line) are connected to each house, composing an energy network. In the operation of the distributed system, a fuel system (reformed gas piping) is added to these networks, and each network follows an objective function in cooperation with other. Because the energy network examined in this section has a short electric transmission distance, there is little energy loss of power transmission compared with the heat transport. However, it is more advantageous regarding energy cost to have improved power transmission loss rather than heat transport, because energy unit prices differ. On the other hand, in an energy network with large heat demand of buildings in a cold region, such as houses and apartments, office buildings and hospitals, heat transport loss has large effect on energy cost and system efficiency. Until now, the distributed installation planning of cogeneration using a genetic algorithm has been investigated [15]. Also in this report, the cost of heat transport and the problem of efficiency are pointed out. It is considered that a lot of heat transport using hot-water piping requires route planning of the piping taking heat loss into account. Then, an exploratory program of the piping route that has the minimum amount of heat radiation was developed concerning the hot-water piping of a fuel cell network [14]. With this program, the optimum piping route of the central system and distributed system can be sought. In the last report, it turned out that the heat release of the hot-water piping route of the optimized distributed system is greatly reduced compared with the central system. Therefore, this section considers the route planning of hot-water piping that takes into consideration the load fluctuation of each house connected to the fuel cell network as the next step. Furthermore, this section also considers the influence of the route planning of hot-water piping when connecting solar module equipment to the output changes of the fuel cell network. Moreover, a PEM (proton exchange membrane) fuel cell network is installed into an urban area model in Sapporo, and the optimum hot-water piping route is analyzed. The optimum piping route in winter, summer and mid-term is analyzed, and heat releases are also investigated.

FUEL CELL NETWORK AND ENERGY BALANCE

Fuel Cell Network

Figure 12 shows the equipment model of the distributed system that installs a fuel cell in each building and supplies power and heat to each building through an energy network. On the other hand, a fuel cell and common auxiliary machinery are installed in a machinery room, and the method of supplying electric power and heat through the energy network is described as the central system. In the case of the central system, the heat energy system (hot-water piping) and power system (power transmission line) of each building are connected. In the case of the distributed system, in addition to these, the fuel system (reformed gas piping) of a fuel cell is also connected. A heat transfer medium is flowed for the hot-water network of both systems, and waste heat recovery of the fuel cells and heat supply for each building are attained. Although the route setting of hot-water piping can be arbitrarily planned in this section, the flow of the heat transfer medium is one way. As shown in Figure 12 (b), a city gas reformer (7), a water separator removing water from reformed gas (8), a reformed gas compressor (9), a cylinder (10), a heat storage tank (11), and a back-up boiler (12) are installed in the machinery room of the distributed system. The fuel cell exhaust heat of each building is first supplied to the same building in the distributed system. When there is excess or insufficient heat, it corresponds by operating a heat storage tank and an auxiliary boiler through the network. On one side, the equipment installed in the machinery room of the central system is a fuel cell other than a reformer, a heat storage tank, and a back-up boiler. A header ((4) and (5)) is installed in each building of the central system and the distributed system. Space heating and hot water supply in a building are performed through a radiator and heat exchanger (3) connected to the header.

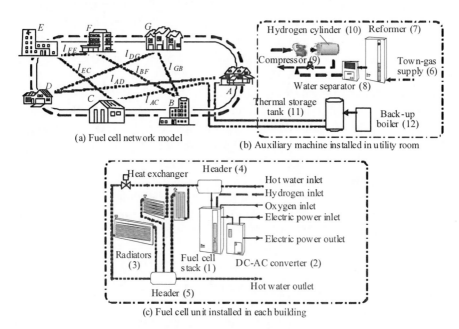

(a) Fuel cell network model

(b) Auxiliary machine installed in utility room

(c) Fuel cell unit installed in each building

Figure 12. Distributed system of the fuel cell network.

Heat Release Model of Hot-Water Piping

Figure 13 shows the model of (a) the hot-water piping route, (b) capacity of the fuel cell placed in each Building, (c) change of hot water temperature and (d) piping heat release per unit length of both systems of the fuel cell network. In these models, both systems install a machinery room in Building A, and a heat transfer medium flows in the order of Building A, B, C, D, E, F, G and A as shown in Figure 13 (a). As shown in Figure 13 (b), a fuel cell is installed in Building A in the central system. In addition, a fuel cell of arbitrary capacity is installed in Buildings A to G in the distributed system. As shown in Figure 13 (c), in the central system, hot water is inputted into Building A with inlet temperature $T_{A,in,t}$. Because hot water has input from the fuel cell exhaust heat, heat storage tank, and auxiliary boiler, it rises to temperature $T_{A,out,t}$ and is released from Building A. The hot water temperature of the central system drops to $T_{A,in,t}$ due to the heat demand of Buildings B-G as well as the heat release of the piping. Moreover, hot water returns to the machinery room in Building A. In the central system, since the hot water temperature falls in the order of Buildings A to G, the difference in the temperature of the outside air and the hot water becomes small. Therefore, as shown in Figure 13 (d), the heat release per unit length of the piping becomes small. Compared with this, in the distributed system, the outlet hot water temperature of each building is decided by the balance of hot water, input quantity of heat to each building, the amount of exhaust heat of the fuel cell installed in the building, and the heat demand of the building. Therefore, the outlet hot water temperature of each building fluctuates as shown in Figure 13 (c). As a result, the heat release per unit length of piping also fluctuates as shown in Figure 13 (d). Therefore, the sum of heat release changes with the building order that the hot-water piping passes.

Output Characteristics of the Fuel Cell

The model of the PEM fuel cell load factor, and the heat output and power load are shown in Figure 14. However, the power output is a value of the AC-DC converter outlet, and the heat output is a value of the fuel cell outlet. In the analysis case described in after Section, the fuel cell capacity of the central system and the distributed system is determined to be 1.2 times the maximum power load. The load factor of the fuel cell at an arbitrary time is calculable from the power generation capacity described above, and the power load. In addition, if the load factor of the fuel cell is given to Figure 14, the heat output ($H_{f,m,t}$ of Equation (13) in the following section) of the fuel cell is calculable.

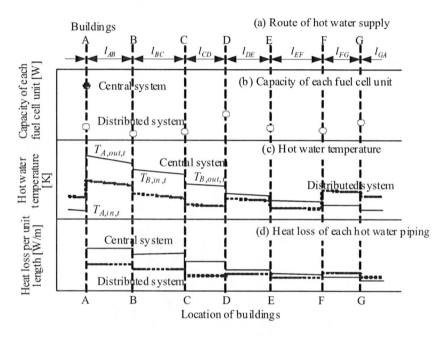

Figure 13. Arrangement plan of fuel cell units.

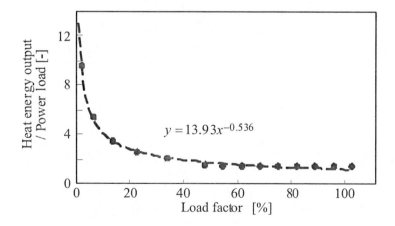

Figure 14. Cell performance.

Energy Balance Equation

The number of buildings connected to a network was set at N, and a total of M_f fuel cells generated electricity in sampling time t ($N \geq M_f$ and $M_f = 1$ in the central system). At this time, the power balance is expressed with Equation (12) and the heat balance is expressed with Equation (13).

$$\sum_{m=1}^{M_f} E_{f,m,t} = \sum_{n=1}^{N} E_{need,n,t} + \sum_{v=1}^{V} \Delta E_{sub,v,t} \tag{12}$$

$$\sum_{m=1}^{M_f} H_{f,m,t} + H_{st,t} + H_{bo,t} = \sum_{n=1}^{N} H_{need,n,t} + \sum_{n=1}^{N} \Delta H_{hw,nn',t} \tag{13}$$

S : Single-person household
D : Family household (2 persons)
F : Family household (3 ~ 4 persons)
DH : Two household house (5 or more persons)
SO : Small office
CS : Convenience store
AP : Apartment house

?AP(1) : AP2, AP4
  6 houses (single person? 1, two persons? 2, three persons? 2, four persons? 1)
?AP(2) : AP3, AP6
  8 houses (single persons? 3, two persons? 2, three persons? 2, four persons? 1)
?AP(3) : AP1, AP5
  10 houses (single persons? 10)

Figure 15. Urban area model.

The left-hand side of Equation (12) expresses the power in the AC-DC converter outlet of a total of M_f fuel cells in the generating mode. Moreover, the

2nd term of the right-hand side expresses the power consumption of V number of auxiliary machines V (reformed gas compressor, hot-water circulating pump, etc.). The 1st term of the left-hand side of Equation (13) expresses the exhaust heat of fuel cells, and the 2nd term and the 3rd term express the heat output of the heat storage tank and back-up boiler, respectively. Moreover, the 2nd term of the right-hand side expresses the heat release of the hot-water piping surface that connects each building. $\Delta H_{hw,nn',t}$ expresses the heat release from hot-water piping that connects Building n to Building n', and is calculated from Equation (14). This section assumes the installation of hot-water piping on the ground. However, underground piping etc. is analyzable by the same calculation. In the analysis case in after Section, in order to make the hot-water flow rate in the piping 1 m/s or less, the piping inside diameter was 60 mm. Around the hot-water piping is equipped with a 40-mm-thick polystyrene-foam heat insulating mold. Moreover, the overall heat transfer coefficient ($\overline{h}$ in Equation (14)) between the hot water in the piping and outside air is calculated as 8.0 W/m^2 K.

$$\Delta H_{hw,nn',t} = \overline{h} \cdot \pi \cdot D_p \cdot l_{nn'} \cdot (T_{n,out,t} - T_{atm,t}) \tag{14}$$

Urban Area Model and Energy Demand Pattern

Figure 15 shows an urban area model in Sapporo assuming application of the fuel cell network. The number of the buildings of this urban area model is 74. This is separated into 16 buildings in Area 1, 23 buildings in Area 2, 13 buildings in Area 3, 12 buildings in Area 4, and 10 buildings in Area 5. The energy network is constructed for each Area. The usages of a building are a single-person household (S: the symbols correspond to Figure 15), a two-person household (D), a three- to four-person household (F), two households living together comprising five or more persons (DH), a small office (SO), a 24-hour convenience store (CS) and an apartment house (AP). The apartment house is a scheme of six households (AP2 and AP4 in Figure 15), eight households (AP3 and AP6), and ten households (AP1 and AP5). The power and heat demand pattern of each building in winter, summer, and mid-term are shown in Figure 16 [16-18]. Note that the number of household members differs in the apartment house in Figures 16 (e) to (g). Figure 17 shows the total amount of power and heat demand on each representative day in Area 1 to Area 5.

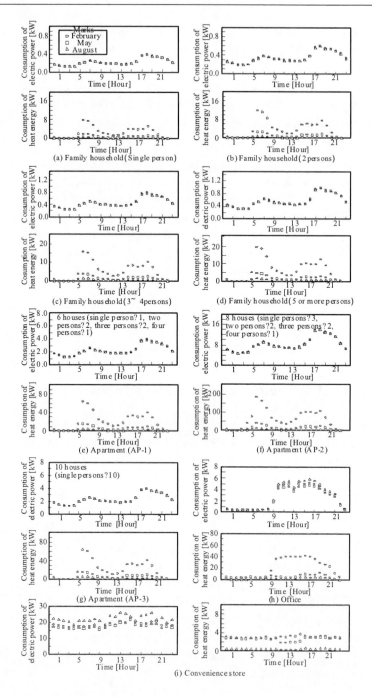

Figure 16. Energy demand patterns.

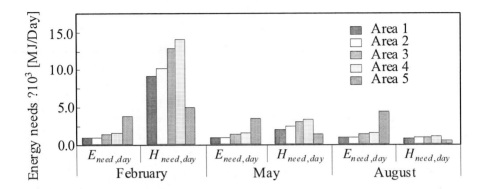

Figure 17. Energy needs for each area.

ROUTE PLANNING METHOD OF PIPING

Route Planning Method of Piping Using the TSP (Traveling Salesman Problem [19])

The chromosome model indicating the piping route is installed into the general genetic algorithm, and gene manipulation, such as crossover and mutation, is added. In this case, many routes that pass the same building two or more times, and route solutions that do not pass some buildings are obtained. Since such routes cannot be managed, all of these chromosome models will be canceled and their analysis efficiency is very low. So, in this section, the view of route order expression by Dewdney is installed [20]. According to this view, although each gene model expresses the building number of each building, this number is not an actual number but the listed number of a building. If this listed number method is installed, since the chromosome model that should be canceled will not appear, analysis efficiency will improve.

The optimal solution to the route searching problem of hot-water piping is a route with minimum heat release of the piping. Therefore, the fitness value of the genetic algorithm is evaluated highly, so that the value of the objective function shown in Equation (15) is small.

$$F_O = \sum_{t=1}^{Period} \sum_{n=1}^{N} \Delta H_{hw,nn',t} \tag{15}$$

Analysis Flow of the Search Program of the Piping Route

The analysis procedure of the route planning is described below. Each item of data of the coordinate and the usage of each building in the urban area model shown in Figure 15, the energy need pattern shown in Figure 16, and the outside air temperature of a representative day of every month shown in Figure 18 is given to the analysis program. Next, two or more random chromosome models indicating the route order described in this Section are prepared. For each of these chromosome models, the fitness shown in Equation (15) is evaluated, and models of high fitness are proliferated, and low models are screened. Furthermore, crossover and mutation are added to the remaining chromosome models, and such fitnesses are evaluated. These calculations are repeated only the number of times (equal to a generation number) decided beforehand. Moreover, the model with fitness maximum is chosen among the last generation's chromosome model groups. The optimal solution is the piping route expressed by this chromosome model. Heat release $\Delta H_{hw,nn',t}$ of the connection piping in Equation (15) is calculated using the following procedure. Power demand $E_{need,n,t}$ at a certain sampling time is obtained from the power demand pattern of each building. Before Section "Output characteristics of the fuel cell" describes the capacity and output characteristics of the fuel cell placed in each building. Heat output $E_{need,n,t}$ when operating the fuel cell according to the power demand pattern can be obtained from Equation (12). Fuel cell exhaust heat $H_{f,m,t}$ is calculated for every building in the distributed system. The fuel cell exhaust heat of the fuel cell installed in the machinery room in the central system is calculated. Both systems set the hot water temperature of the machinery room outlet to 353 K, and calculate piping heat release $\Delta H_{hw,nn',t}$ from Equation (14) using the piping specification described in before Section "Energy balance equation". Moreover, a back-up boiler is operated so that the hot water temperature of the heat storage tank outlet may become 353 K. The temperature of the hot water that returns to the heat storage tank through the hot-water network shall be about 333 K, and the amount of hot-water circulating flow is decided. Heat input-and-output $H_{st,t}$ of the heat storage tank is calculated by giving $H_{f,m,t}$, $\Delta H_{hw,nn',t}$, and heat demand $H_{need,n,t}$ of each building to Equation (13). When the amount of heat storage run short, the heat of $H_{bo,t}$ is outputted from the boiler.

Figure 19 shows the heat balance model of the hot-water piping network. Connecting Buildings A to G with piping in order, hot water returns to Building

A. The machinery room is set in Building A and the heat storage tank and the back-up boiler are installed, and each heat output is $H_{st,t}$ and $H_{bo,t}$. Buildings A to G have heat demands $H_{need,A,t}$ to $H_{need,G,t}$, respectively. The distributed system has exhaust heat power output $H_{f,A,t}$ to $H_{f,G,t}$ with a fuel cell installed in each building. In the case of the central system, there is exhaust heat power $H_{f,A,t}$ from the fuel cell installed in Building A. In order to estimate heat release $\Delta H_{hw,nn',t}$ ($n = A, B, C,....., G$) from the piping that connects each building, it is necessary to give the outside air temperature $T_{atm,t}$ to Equation (14). So, in the analysis case of next Section, the meteorological data of Sapporo in summer (August), winter (February), and mid-term (May) shown in Figure 18 are used [21].

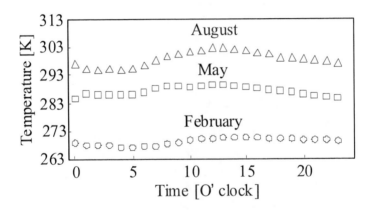

Figure 18. Outside temperature model in Sapporo.

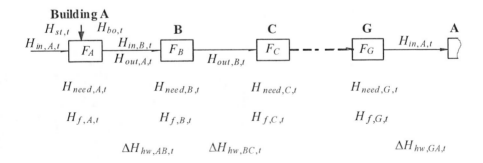

Figure 19. Heat energy network model.

CASE STUDY

Program Check by Shortest Route Search

The analytic accuracy of the route planning program of piping developed in this section is checked. Therefore, the shortest route for the urban area model in Figure 15 is sought. This analysis result is shown in Figure 20. In the result in Figure 20, the hot-water piping of all the areas is a closed route. It was checked using the analysis method of TSP by Dewdney that these route results were the shortest in length [20]. Moreover, the variable installed in the genetic algorithm was changed variously, and numerical simulation was repeated. The chromosome model with a population of 2500, a crossover probability of 0.9, a mutation probability of 0.001, and a generation number of 200 had the best analysis efficiency of computation time and accuracy.

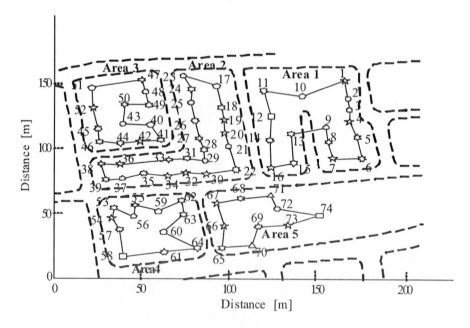

Figure 20. Results of minimum length route analysis.

Power Generation Capacity of a Fuel Cell

In the central system, a machinery room is set in Building 1 in Area 1 as shown in Figure 20, Building 17 in Area 2, Building 40 in Area 3, Building 53 in Area 4, and Building 65 in Area 5, and a fuel cell is installed in each building. The power generation capacity of the fuel cells is set at 26 kW, 26 kW, 36 kW, 42 kW, and 78 kW, respectively, according to the method described in before Section "Output characteristics of the fuel cell". Moreover, the fuel cell capacity of the distributed system was also decided to be values of Table 7 according to same Section.

Table 7. Fuel cell capacity of buildings

Mark	Maximum electricity needs (kW)	Fuel cell capacity (kW)
S	0.4	0.5
D	0.8	1.0
F	0.9	1.1
DH	1.0	1.2
SO	6.0	7.5
CS	26.0	32
AP(1)	4.0	5.0
AP(2)	14.0	20.0
AP(3)	4.0	5.0

Result of Route Planning

(1) Difference Between a Distributed System and a Central System

Figures 21 and 22 show the route planning results of a representative day in winter, summer, and mid-term of the distributed system and the central system, respectively. The piping routes of each Area in Figures 21 and 22 differ from the shortest routes shown in Figure 20. This is because the heat release changes with the piping route as before Section "Heat release model of hot-water piping" and Figure 13 explain. In particular, the analysis result of Area 5 in Figures 21 (a) to (c) greatly differs from the shortest route shown in Figure 20. In this area, power

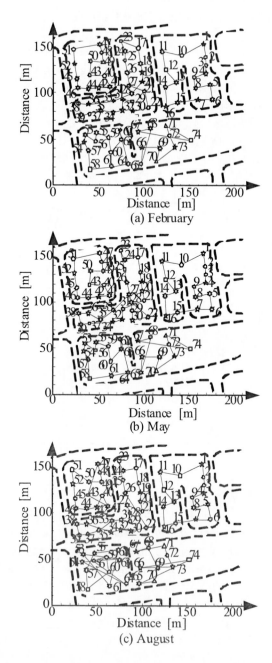

(a) February

(b) May

(c) August

Figure 21. Results of hot-water pipe route analysis of distributed system.

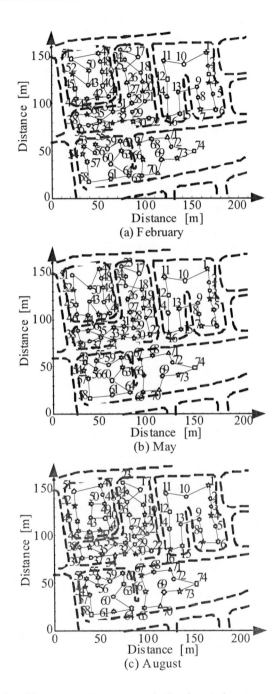

(a) February

(b) May

(c) August

Figure 22. Results of hot-water pipe route analysis of central system.

consumption is large compared with the surrounding buildings. However, two convenience stores (Buildings 70 and 71) with little heat consumption are included. The exhaust heat of the fuel cells installed in these two buildings becomes surplus in the distributed system. Correspondence of this analysis program when there is large heat surplus is not taken into consideration because the analytic accuracy of the route planning falls. Compared with this, in the analysis result of the piping route of the central system shown in Figure 22, large heat surplus is not generated on the route. Therefore, compared with the result of Area 5 in the distributed system, the result of the central system is close to the shortest route.

Figure 23 shows the ratio of the heat release of the hot-water piping to the heat demand of the central system and the distributed system. When the distributed system and the central system are compared regarding the piping heat release of each area, the heat release of the distributed system is about 25% of the central system (Area 4 on a representative day in August) at maximum. Moreover, when the heat release of all the areas in each season is added, the distributed system is about 75% of the central system. Therefore, if optimization analysis is installed into the route planning problem of the hot-water piping network, it is possible to greatly reduce heat release. The heat release in the case of the shortest piping length shown in Figure 20 for reference was calculated. As a result, the heat demand amount was almost the same as heat release in both systems.

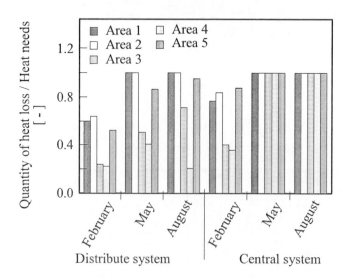

Figure 23. Heat loss of piping.

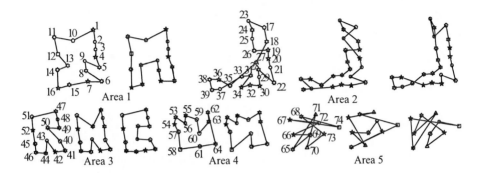

Figure 24. Results of hot-water pipe route analysis of distributed system with load fluctuation of 15% in February.

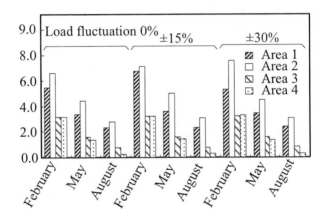

Figure 25. Heat loss with load fluctuations.

(2) Route Planning of Hot-Water Piping with Load Fluctuation

The result of the route analysis in the distributed system when adding less than ±15% random load fluctuation to the power and heat demand pattern on a winter representative day is shown in Figure 24. However, the route patterns shown here do not comprise all of the results. If the analysis that added load fluctuation is repeated, several different route patterns will appear in any area. Moreover, Figure 25 shows the result of the hot-water piping heat release of these analyses. When ±30% or less load fluctuation is added, the heat release is changed from -19% to 3% in the range to an analysis result without load fluctuation, and this is averaged at -6%. In this way, if load fluctuation occurs, heat release will drop. Furthermore, when fluctuation is added to a small power load, a no-load condition will occur.

Piping Route Plan with a Solar Module

The influence of a hot-water piping route plan when connecting solar module equipment to the power network of the distributed system is investigated. The solar module equipment is 24 m^2 in the power generation module area, and the power output of the AC-DC converter outlet is a maximum of 3.0 kW. Figure 26 shows the power generation characteristic model in Sapporo for solar module equipment [17]. The random output change within ±25% and ±50% is added to Figure 26, and these data are used for analysis. The power obtained by the solar module is supplied to each building through the power network. Since each fuel cell connected to the network differs at each load factor, the generation efficiency of each fuel cell is different. Consequently, the fuel cell is stopped when generation efficiency is low instead of using solar power.

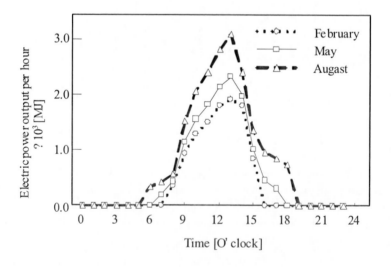

Figure 26. solar mocdule output.

Figure 27 shows the analysis results when adding less than ±30% random load fluctuation to the power and heat demand on a representative day in winter, and adding less than ±25% random solar power. As before Section describes, if analysis is repeated, two or more route results will appear in all the areas. Since some fuel cells stop if solar module equipment is connected to the network, compared with Figure 24, the piping routes may differ greatly.

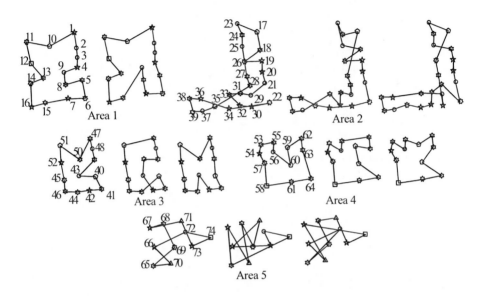

Figure 27. Result of hot-water pipe rout analysis of distributed system with load fluctuation of +/- 30% and solar power output fluctuation of +/- 25% in February.

Figure 28 shows the result of the heat release of hot-water piping when the fluctuation rate of the power and heat load is less than ±30%, and the output change rates of the solar module are less than ±25% and less than ±50%. Compared with solar power with ±25% output change, the result of the heat release with ±50% output change is -16% to 5%. The average reduction value of heat release is 2%. Moreover, if solar module equipment is connected to the network, compared with when it is not connected, heat release fluctuation of -7% to 1% will occur. The average heat release is reduced by 2%. If power is supplied to the network from solar module equipment, some of the fuel cells connected to the network will stop. As a result, the fuel cell exhaust heat outputted to the hot-water network decreases, and heat release decreases. In this case, the capacity of solar module equipment is small and heat release reduction of the hot-water piping is about 2%. However, if the capacity of the solar module connected to the network is extended, the heat release of the hot-water piping will become smaller.

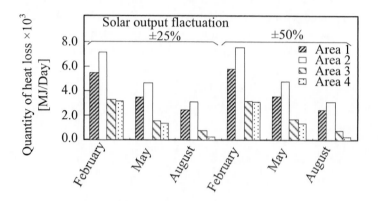

Figure 28. Heat loss with load fluctuation 30% and solar device outputs.

CONCLUSION

A route planning program that optimizes the hot-water piping route of a fuel cell energy network was developed. The view of TSP is installed into the analysis program, and the fuel cell central system and fuel cell distributed system can be examined. An urban area model of 74 buildings in Sapporo was analyzed, and the piping route and the hot-water piping heat release were investigated. Furthermore, the piping route and heat release of the fuel cell network that connected the buildings with load fluctuation and solar module equipment with output fluctuation were examined. As a result, the piping heat release in one year from the distributed system is about 75% compared to the central system. The piping heat release with power load fluctuation of ±30% shows an average of a 6% reduction compared with no load fluctuation. This is because a fuel cell idle state of load zero will occur if the load is varied when the power demand is small. Moreover, compared with when solar module equipment is not connected, there is an average 2% reduction of heat release at the time of ±50% output change of the solar module equipment. This is because some of the distributed fuel cells are stopped due to the power supply to the solar module network. Although hot-water piping with an inside diameter of 60 mm was assumed in this section, a reduced size is actually taken.

Chapter 3

LOAD LEVELING OF FUEL CELL SYSTEM BY OXYGEN CONCENTRATION CONTROL OF CATHODE GAS

INTRODUCTION

Wide usage of proton exchange membrane fuel cells (PEFC) in houses, as well as in small to middle-scale buildings requires a fuel cell stack, a reformer, a heat storage tank, and cost reduction of cost of a back-up heat source. In particular, the fuel cell stack is expensive, and is therefore used together with commercial power and requires a device for reducing the power generation capacity. Furthermore, if a fuel cell system is installed with a large load fluctuation with a town gas reformer in a house and performs load-following operation, partial load operation will occur frequently [22-24]. The dynamic characteristics of a fuel cell stack and a reformer differ greatly, and the load following rate of the reformer is very slow compared to the load following rate of the fuel cell stack [25-25]. If small partial loads occur frequently in short time intervals, a drop in efficiency will be expected for the reformer with a slow speed of response. The time shift of the electric-power supply and demand using a battery as a possible method to solve the reduction in fuel cell capacity and the dynamic characteristics of the reformer can be considered. However, when the cost of a battery, its charge-and-discharge efficiency, and its life are taken into consideration, the introduction of the battery system to a house with long operation time has many considerations. Improvement in the electric-power-generation capacity reduction of a fuel cell and partial load operation of a reformer has been attempted by electric power generation in time shifts using hydrogen and oxygen produced by water electrolysis using surplus electric power.

Although reformed gas and air are supplied and power generation from the fuel cell is performed in time zones with little electric power demand, the power also has to be supplied to a water electrolyzer. The hydrogen and oxygen produced by water electrolysis and they are stored under compression in cylinders. On the other hand, electric power demand supplies and generates the gases in the gas cylinders to the fuel cell during a time zone with larger demand. The electric-power-generation characteristics of PEFC improve by supplying a higher concentration of oxygen to the cathode [29-32]. Therefore, hydrogen and oxygen are produced during time zones of smaller electric power demand, and the power load peak is leveled by using these gases for time zones of greater electric power demand. Although the capacity of the fuel cell stack has been decided until now using the output characteristics of the fuel cell at the time of electricity generation with reformed gas and air, in the operational method that will be proposed in this report, the capacity of the fuel cell stack can be decided from the output characteristics at the time of electricity generation with hydrogen and oxygen. In this case, since the electric-power-generation characteristics of the fuel cell improve by supplying gas and pure oxygen with a high oxygen concentration to the cathode compared with the case where just air is supplied, the cell stack capacity can be reduced. The proton exchange membrane water electrolysis system (SPE) for water electrolysis has an efficiency of 84% at 393K and 0.4MPa, and has already been established as a basic standard technology. Moreover, the SPE system cost may also reduce substantially in the future [9, 33].

In the present study, the capacity of the fuel cell facility, the town gas consumption and the operational time of auxiliary machines is investigated by assuming the introduction of a fuel cell system with a water electrolyzer into an energy-demand model of a house, a hospital, a factory, a hotel, and a small store for 24-hour operation. These models are used as analysis examples.

SYSTEM DESCRIPTION

System Structure

Figure 29 shows the structural drawing of a fuel cell system assuming water electrolysis. Town gas fuel of a fuel cell system is supplied to the heat source burner (BN) and reforming gas system (RM) of a reformer. Town gas is reformed by a reformer, and a dryer (DY) recovers the surplus water of reforming gas after that. After removing the carbon monoxide in reforming gas with a carbon monoxide oxidization device (MC), the anode of the fuel cell (FC) is supplied. If power is supplied to a water electrolyzer (EL) when the power load of the system is small, hydrogen and oxygen are generated. The hydrogen generated by water electrolysis other than reforming gas can be supplied to the anode of the fuel cell. The air of a blower (B_3) or pure oxygen generated with EL can be supplied to the cathode of a fuel cell. Power is supplied from the system to the demand-side using a fuel cell system $E_{IT,t}$ or a commercial power system $E_{cm,t}$ using an interconnection device. Part of the electric power generated using the fuel cell is supplied to a water electrolyzer, and the electric power $\Delta E_{EL,t}$ is consumed for the production of hydrogen and oxygen. The hydrogen and oxygen thus produced are compressed into gas cylinders CDH and CDO, and are stored. The power consumption of the compressors are $\Delta E_{PH,t}$ and $\Delta E_{PO,t}$, respectively. The stored gases can be supplied to the fuel cell and electric power generation, which shifted the time period, can be carried out. The exhaust heat of a fuel cell is stored in a heat storage tank (ST) by the heat transfer medium conveyed with a pump (PP). When there is exhaust heat input exceeding the capacity of the heat storage tank, a part for surplus is released from a radiator (RA). In addition, heat is supplied to the demand side by feeding tap water to the heat exchanger installed within the ST.

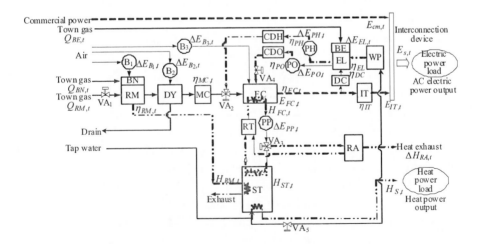

Figure 29. Structure of fuel cell cogeneration with electrolyzer.

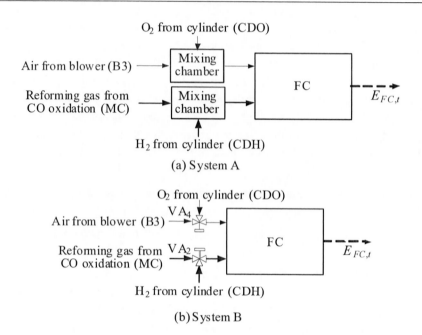

(a) System A

(b) System B

Figure 30. Structure of fuel cell cogeneration with battery.

Figure 30 shows the two methods of supplying hydrogen and oxygen to a fuel cell stack. In Figure 30 (a), hydrogen and reformed gas from a gas cylinder are mixed in one chamber, oxygen from a gas cylinder and air from the blower B_3 are mixed in another chamber, and the system supplying these gases to the fuel cell stack is described as System A. Since the cathode gas in System A uses mixed air and oxygen, the oxygen concentration supplied to the fuel cell varies. On the other hand, in Figure 30 (b), valves VA_2 and VA_4 are operated, and the anode gas and cathode gas which are supplied to the fuel cell stack are changed. This system is termed as system B. Since the air flow path of the blower B_3 and the flow path of the gas cylinder oxygen are changed, and cathode gas is supplied to the fuel cell, air or pure oxygen will be supplied. In System A of Figure 30 (a), the hydrogen supplied to FC is a mixed gas of MC and CDH. Moreover, the oxygen supplied to FC is a mixed gas of B_3 and CDO. In this case, since the air of B_3 and the oxygen of CDO are mixed and FC is supplied, the oxygen concentration changes. On the other hand, VA_2 and VA_4 of System B of Figure 30 (b) are switching valves. Therefore, VA_2 supplies the gas of MC or CDH to FC. Moreover, VA_4 supplies the gas of B_3 or CDO to FC. The electrochemical reaction of the cathode in the case of supplying the gas of CDO to FC uses pure oxygen, and the electrochemical reaction of the cathode in the case of supplying the gas of B_3 to FC uses air. Although the oxygen concentration in the cathode gas of System A is controllable, the oxygen supplied to cathode from CDO is pure gas in the case of System B. However, even if it mixes the air of B_3 and pure oxygen of CDO of System A, since the volume of gas other than oxygen is large, the oxygen concentration cannot be increases. Since the power-generation characteristics of the fuel cell especially using pure oxygen improves compared with the fuel cell using air, it is the target to reduce the fuel cell capacity greatly by supplying at a peak period. System A and System B attempt a reduction in power-generation capacity by increasing the oxygen concentration in the gas supplied to the cathode, shifting time and supplying this gas to a fuel cell. However, System A and System B are independent structures, and combined operation is not considered. Although the operating methods of the cathode gas of each system differ by power load, the details are described later.

Town gas is supplied to the burner BN with quantity of flow $Q_{BN,t}$, and the heat source of the reformer RM is acquired. Electricity consumption is $\Delta E_{B_1,t}$ though air is supplied to a burner by the blower B_1. Moreover, air is supplied to the dryer DY, which is used for removing water from the reformed gas, by the blower B_2, and electricity consumption is $\Delta E_{B_2,t}$. The blower, which supplies air to the fuel cell stack, is B_3 and the electricity consumption is $\Delta E_{B_3,t}$. For heat recovery from the fuel cell stack, electric power $\Delta E_{PP,t}$ is consumed using the heat-transfer-medium circulated by pump PP. Although hydrogen and oxygen produced by water electrolysis are stored in each gas cylinder with operation of compressors PH and PO. The electric power consumed by the compressors are $\Delta E_{PH,t}$ and $\Delta E_{PO,t}$ respectively. The electricity consumption $\Delta E_{B_1,t}$, $\Delta E_{B_2,t}$, and $\Delta E_{B_3,t}$ of the blowers B_1, B_2, and B_3, and the electricity consumption $\Delta E_{PP,t}$ of the pump PP are obtained from the electric power supplied from a commercial power system. The electricity consumption $\Delta E_{PH,t}$ and $\Delta E_{PO,t}$ of the compressors PH and PO are supplied by the electric power generated by the fuel cell. The system shown in Figure 29 is electric power generation system, and the thermal output system is not taken into consideration.

Fuel Cell Performance

Figure 31 shows the cell performance curve for an operating temperature of 333 K, with the gas pressure at the anode and cathode being 0.1MPa [29, 30]. Although the cell efficiency changes with oxygen concentration of the cathode gas, there is no difference in the cell efficiency whether reformed gas or hydrogen is supplied to the anode.

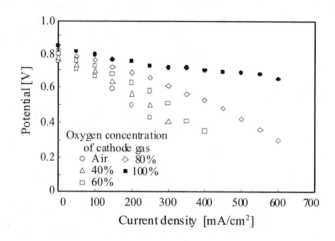

Figure 31. Cell performance generated with oxygen. Operating temperature 333K, and reactant flow stoichiometries 2 both hydrogen and oxygen.

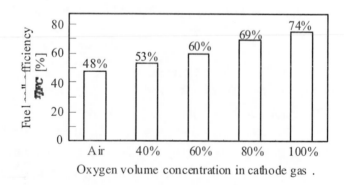

Figure 32. Efficiency of the fuel cell electric power output. Operating temperature 333K, and pressure 0.1 MPa.

Figure 32 shows the model of the generation efficiency η_{FC} of the fuel cell stack [29, 30]. When pure oxygen is supplied to the cathode, the efficiency is 1.54

times that of the case when air is supplied. When the electrode surface of an anode and cathode is 1 m^2, Figure 33 shows the model of the oxygen concentration supplied to the cathode, the town gas consumption, and the power output in an inverter outlet [23, 24, 29, 30]. However, these characteristics are the models when setting the reformer efficiency η_{RM} to be constant at 73%. Details of η_{RM} are given below.

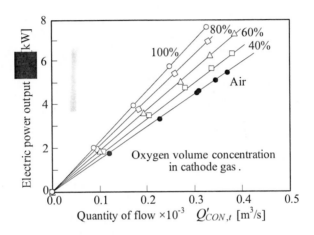

Figure 33. The power output of inverter by difference in the oxygen volume concentration in cathode gas. The area of the electrode of anode and cathode of the fuel cell stack is 1 m^2, respectively. Reformer efficiency is 0.73.

System Operation

The operational model of the fuel cell system with water electrolysis is shown in Figure 34. In the fuel cell system, reformed gas and air are supplied and the threshold value E_{set} of the electric power shown in the figure is generated. However, during the time period when the power load $E_{d,t}$ is less than E_{set}, the electric power of ($E_{set} - E_{d,t}$) is supplied to the water electrolyzer. The hydrogen and the oxygen, which are produced in this time period, are compressed and stored in the gas cylinders. As shown in Figures 32 and 33, the output characteristics of the cell stack improve by supplying gas with a high oxygen concentration to the cathode rather than supplying air. Then, the threshold value E_{set} of the electric power is compared with the power load $E_{d,t}$, and the hydrogen and oxygen stored in the gas cylinders using $E_{d,t}$ in the large time period are supplied to the cell stack. The hydrogen and the oxygen stored in the gas cylinders are supplied to the fuel cell by either of the two systems shown in Figure 30. With the operating method described in the Figure 34, the power generation characteristics under a high load serves as a high output compared with the power generation method with conventional reformed gas and air, and can perform peak-cut of the electric power load. The installed capacity of the conventional fuel cell stack was decided by the electrode surface product which can output the maximum value of electric power demand at the time of generating electricity with reformed gas and air. In this study, at the time of low load, hydrogen and oxygen are produced by water electrolysis using surplus electric power, and a reduction in capacity of the cell stack is attempted by generating electricity with this hydrogen and oxygen at the time of high load including at the maximum value of the power load.

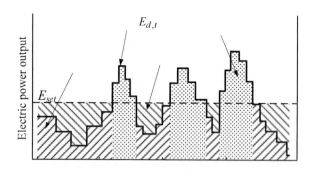

Figure 34. System operation.

The operating range of the reformer is limited by always operating the fuel cell system at the electric-power threshold value E_{set}. In this case, consideration of partial load operation for which the efficiency of the reformer falls, and consideration of the delay time of the speed of response of the load are avoidable.

Although steam reforming of the town gas quantity of flow $Q_{RM,t}$ is carried out and reformed gas is produced in the reformer, the heat source for reforming reaction burns and obtains using the town gas with a flow quantity of $Q_{BN_1,t}$. The following equation defines the reformer efficiency and the maximum of this value is 73% [9].

$$\eta_{RM} = \frac{W_H}{(W_C + W_R)} \cdot 100 \tag{16}$$

With CO oxidation equipment, when burning and changing CO in the reformed gas into CO_2, a part of the hydrogen also burns. Nearly 2% of hydrogen in the reformed gas will burn with CO oxidation equipment, with an associated efficiency η_{MC} of 98%. Therefore, the hydrogen flow quantity $Q_{MC,H_2,t}$ of the CO oxidization equipment outlet and the town gas flow quantity ($Q_{CON,t} = Q_{RM,t} + Q_{BN_1,t}$) supplied to the reformer are connected by the following equation.

$$Q_{MC,H_2,t} = \eta_{MC,t} \cdot \eta_{RM} \cdot Q_{CON,t} \tag{17}$$

Water Electrolysis

Water electrolysis produces hydrogen and oxygen using the proton exchange membrane electrolysis system [9]. The pure water used for water electrolysis supplies and produces tap water which carries out heat exchange to a pure-water production device inside the heat storage tank. A charcoal filter and an ion exchange filter are installed by the pure-water production device, and electric power is not consumed for its operation. Moreover, the cost of pure-water production, which uses a charcoal filter and an ion exchange filter, is inexpensive. Water electrolysis is performed under conditions of 393K and 0.4MPa, heat source burns and obtains town gas by the flow quantity of $Q_{BN_2,t}$, and makes town gas a heat source. The efficiency η_{EL} of water electrolysis is 84% [9], and the direct-current power generated with the fuel cell is supplied to the water electrolyzer through a DC-DC converter (efficiency η_{DC} =95%). The hydrogen and oxygen produced by water electrolysis are compressed using the compressor, and are stored in gas cylinders. The electricity consumption in the hydrogen compressor is calculated by the following equation.

$$\Delta E_{PH,t} = 1/\eta_{CDH} \cdot P_{in} \cdot Q'_{in,t} \cdot \ln(Q'_{in,t}/Q'_{out,t}) \tag{18}$$

Here, $P_{out} = P_{in} \cdot Q'_{in,t}/Q'_{out,t} = 1.0 \text{ MPa}$. The hydrogen compressor-efficiency η_{CDH} is 50%. The electricity consumption $\Delta E_{PO,t}$ in the compressor which compresses oxygen is similarly calculated.

Energy Balance

Equation (19) is the electric-power balance in sampling time t.

$$E_{FC,t} = E_{IT,t}/\eta_{IT} + \Delta E_{EL,t}/\eta_{DC} + \Delta E_{PH,t} + \Delta E_{PO,t} \tag{19}$$

The left side is the power output of a fuel cell stack, and the 1st term on the right hand side is the electric power output to the interconnection device from the inverter and $E_{IT,t}$ is equal to the electric power demand in sampling time t. The 2nd term on the right hand side is the electric power used for the water electrolysis operation, and the 3rd term and 4th terms are the electricity consumption in each compressor used for hydrogen and oxygen. Commercial power is used as the power supply to other blowers and the pump. Equation (20) shows the heat balance of the system. The left side of Equation (20) expresses the heat output from the fuel cell, the reformer, and the heat storage tank, and the right hand side expresses the thermal output from the system. $H_{S,t}$ is equal to the heat demand amount in sampling time t.

$$H_{FC,t} + H_{RM,t} + H_{ST,t} = H_{S,t} \tag{20}$$

Equation (21) shows the mass balance of hydrogen. The left side expresses the hydrogen quantity produced by the water electrolyzer, the hydrogen quantity of flow supplied to the fuel cell from the gas cylinder, and hydrogen quantity of flow from the CO oxidization equipment outlet. The right hand side expresses the hydrogen quantity consumed by the fuel cell. Equation (22) shows the mass balance of oxygen. The left side includes oxygen flow rate produced by the water electrolyzer, oxygen flow rate supplied to the fuel cell from the gas cylinder, and air supplied to the fuel cell by the blowers. The right hand side expresses the amount of oxygen consumed by the fuel cell at sampling time t.

$$Q_{EL,H_2,t} + Q_{CDH,H_2,t} + Q_{MC,H_2,t} = Q_{FC,H_2,t} \tag{21}$$

$$Q_{EL,O_2,t} + Q_{CDO,O_2,t} + Q_{B3,O_2,t} = Q_{FC,O_2,t} \tag{22}$$

Analysis Method

The threshold value E_{set} of the electric power for low load and high load is decided so that the balance of the individual amounts of hydrogen and oxygen produced by water electrolysis at the time period of low loading and the amounts consumed by the fuel cell at the time period of high load can balance. Then, E_{set} is decided below which the maximum electric power output of the system, and the balance of the amounts of hydrogen and oxygen produced during the low loading time period and the high load period is calculated. When the power load $E_{d,t}$ exceeds the threshold value E_{set} of electric power, the anode gas supplied to the fuel cell in System A is the mixed gas of reformed gas hydrogen and the cylinder, and the cathode gas is the mixed gas of oxygen in the air supplied by the blower and the cylinder. However, in System A, suspending the gas supply from the reformed gas and blower, and supplying only the hydrogen and the oxygen from each gas cylinder to the fuel cell can also be chosen. The choice of the method of supplying gas, which mixes gas cylinder hydrogen with reformed gas, and the gas which mixes gas cylinder oxygen with blower air to the fuel cell, and the method of supplying only gas cylinder hydrogen and oxygen is decided based upon minimal consumption of gas cylinder oxygen. On the other hand, when the power load $E_{d,t}$ exceeds the threshold value E_{set} of electric power, electric power generation from the fuel cell in System B is performed with the hydrogen and oxygen supplied from the cylinders. In the numerical calculation which determines E_{set}, the balance of hydrogen and oxygen is calculated by E_{set}, the amount of production of hydrogen and oxygen is excessive, and the value of E_{set} whose difference of the balance is the minimum, is decided as a solution. That is, when $E_{set} > E_{d,t}$, the reformed gas produced by the reformer and the blower air are supplied to the fuel cell. In this case, the power output $E_{IT,t}$ at the inverter outlet in Equation (19) is set to $E_{d,t}$. The electric power consumed by the water electrolyzer is $\Delta E_{EL,t} = (E_{set} - E_{d,t})/\eta_{EL}$ and sets the water electrolysis thermal efficiency to η_{EL}. However, in order to supply the direct-current power generated by the fuel cell to the water, a DC-DC converter is required to adjust the voltage.

The efficiency of this DC-DC converter is set to η_{DC} , and the electric power, $\Delta E_{EL,t}/\eta_{DC}$, is supplied to the water electrolyzer from the fuel cell. If the electric power $\Delta E_{EL,t}$ is decided, the amount $Q_{EL,H_2,t}$ of hydrogen production and the amount $Q_{EL,O_2,t}$ of oxygen production can be calculated. The amounts of hydrogen and oxygen for a sampling time interval of Δt which are stored in cylinders are $Q_{EL,H_2,t} \cdot \Delta t$ and $Q_{EL,O_2,t} \cdot \Delta t$, respectively. The electricity consumption $\Delta E_{PH,t}$ in a compressor is calculated by converting $Q_{EL,H_2,t} \cdot \Delta t$ into the volume rate of flow $Q'_{EL,H_2,t}$, and introducing this into $Q_{in,t}$ in Equation (18). The electricity consumption $\Delta E_{PO,t}$ in the compressor, wherein oxygen compression occurs, is calculated similarly. The electric power $E_{FC,t}$ generated by the fuel cell stack is calculated by introducing appropriate values into each term on the right hand side of Equation (19).

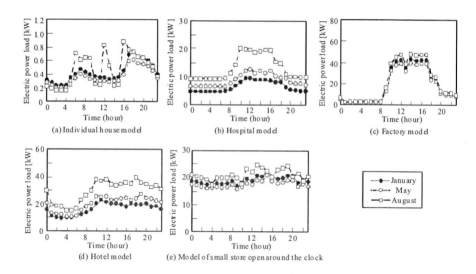

Figure 35. Models of electric power load.

The hydrogen flow quantity $Q_{FC,H_2,t}$ supplied to a fuel cell stack is obtained using Equation (23). The η_{FC} is calculated by creating the approximate expression for the relationship between the oxygen concentration shown in Figure 32 and the efficiency of the fuel cell stack, and introducing the oxygen concentration of the gas supplied to cathode into this approximate expression.

Furthermore, $Q_{MC,H_2,t}$ is calculated from Equation (21), and the town gas flow quantity $Q''_{RM,t} + Q''_{BN,t}$ supplied to a system is calculated by introducing this value into Equation (24).

$$Q'_{FC,H_2,t} = E_{FC,t}/(\alpha \cdot \eta_{FC}) \tag{23}$$

$$Q'_{RM,t} + Q'_{BN,t} = Q'_{MC,H_2,t}/(\eta_{MC} \cdot \eta_{RM}) \tag{24}$$

For $E_{set} < E_{d,t}$, the flow quantities $Q_{CDH,H_2,t}$ and $Q_{CDO,O_2,t}$ are supplied to the fuel cell from the hydrogen and oxygen stored in each gas cylinder. In System A, the oxygen concentration of the cathode gas required to reduce the power load $E_{d,t}$ at sampling time t to E_{set}, is calculated. In order for the oxygen concentration of the gas to be the value described above, the supply oxygen flow rate $Q_{CDO,O_2,t}$ in the gas cylinder added to the oxygen flow rate $Q_{B3,O_2,t}$ in the air supplied by the blower is calculated. The hydrogen flow quantity $Q_{CDH,H_2,t}$ supplied from a gas cylinder is adjusted to be twice the molar flow rate of the oxygen flow rate $Q_{CDO,O_2,t}$. The hydrogen used for the hydrogen flow quantity $Q_{MC,H_2,t}$ in the reformed gas for $Q_{CDH,H_2,t}$ is supplied to the anode of a fuel cell. On the other hand, in System B, the fuel cell is operated only by the cylinder gases, and pure hydrogen and pure oxygen are supplied and generated. The calculation results of the threshold value E_{set} of the electric power should change with the difference in the oxygen concentration of the cathode gas in System A and System B, and differences in the power load pattern introduced into the system.

When $E_{set} = E_{d,t}$ in System A, the reformed gas produced by the reformer and the air from the blower are supplied, and the fuel cell is operated. Water electrolysis is not performed at this time. One of the two methods of operating a fuel cell, (1) with reformed gas and blower air, and (2) with cylinder hydrogen and cylinder oxygen where the value of E_{set} is smaller, is carried out by System B.

CASE STUDY

Weather Conditions in Tokyo

In Tokyo, the annual average temperature for the past five years is 289K. The average temperature in January is 279K, and the highest and the lowest temperatures on a representative day for January are 283K and 275K, respectively. The average temperature in May is 292K, and the highest and the lowest temperatures on a May representative day are 296K and 288K, respectively. The highest and the lowest temperature on a July representative day for the past five years are 302K and 296K, respectively, and the average temperature is 298K [34].

Energy Demand Models

The energy-demand models for an average individual house, a hospital, a factory, a hotel, and a small store with day-long business in Tokyo is shown in Figure 35. Each energy-demand pattern is for a monthly representative day of winter (January), mid-term (May), and summer (August). The space cooling load of all buildings shown in Figure 35 is included in the electric power demand. Although the space heating load of a hospital and a hotel is supplied using the fuel cell exhaust heat, the space heating load of other buildings is included in the electric power demand. The floor space of each building, the energy demand, and the reference capacities of the fuel cell installed in the buildings are shown in Table 8. The power-generation capacity in Table 8 is decided by an increase of nearly 10% in the maximum electric power load of the buildings. In a numerical analysis, as for the electric power generation characteristics of the fuel cell, the relationship shown in Figure 33 needs to be maintained relatively, and the efficiency of the fuel cell stack is obtained by giving oxygen concentration to the approximate expression which determines Figure 32.

The values indicated in Table 9 are used for the efficiencies of the auxiliary machines used in the analysis. The values of such efficiency are products on the market and the products under engineering development.

Table 8. Total floor space, power consumption and fuel cell capacity of each model

Model	Total floor space (m²)	Power consumption of January, May and August (MJ/day)	Fuel cell capacity (kW)
		(Electric power / Heat power)	
(a) Individual house	128	36, 32.4, 39.6 / 77.4, 48.6, 27.0	1.0
(b) Hospital	600	551, 745, 1130 / 3640, 1670, 1280	22.0
(c) Factory	800	1620, 1490, 1800 /	55.0
(d) Hotel	1000	1440, 1760, 2560 / 5220, 3380, 2380	44.0
(e) Small store	145	1660, 1510, 1810 /	28.0

Table 9. The values of the efficiency used for analysis

$\eta_{RM,t}$	$\eta_{MC,t}$	$\eta_{DC,t}$	η_{PH}	η_{PO}	η_{EL}	$\eta_{IT,t}$
73 %	98 %	95 %	50 %	50 %	84 %	95 %

RESULTS AND DISCUSSION

Operation Planning and Fuel Cell Capacity Reduction Effect

Figure 36 shows the calculation results for the operational plan after the introduction of System A into each building, and Figure 37 shows the calculation results of the operational plan after the introduction of System B. In the system which supplies all the electric power loads using the fuel cell, the capacity of the fuel cell was conventionally fixed to be the value which covers the annual peak electricity demand. However, if both System A and System B are introduced, the capacity of the fuel cell can be reduced to a value which covers the electric power load shown overall in Figures 36 and 37. The production of electricity from the fuel cell stack is the value which divides the electric power needs in the figures using the inverter efficiency η_{IT} =0.95. Moreover, for the analysis of the small store in System A, and the hotel and small store in System B, the solution by calculation of a representative day in August was not obtained. This is because the amount of oxygen required for the peak-cut of electric power load cannot be produced by water electrolysis in the time zones when power load is small.

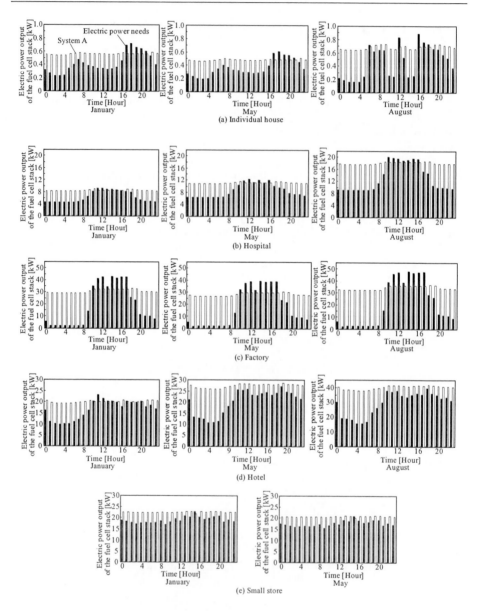

Figure 36. Operation planning of system A.

The analysis results for the conventional System A and the System B are shown in Table 10 for the electric power output supplying the biggest load for each sampling time of every month for representative days in winter (January), mid-term (May), and summer (August), as the power generation capacity of the fuel cell. In System A, improvements in the fuel cell efficiency by increasing the oxygen concentration as shown in Figures 32 and 33, can be performed at the time of the high load of $E_{d,t} > E_{set}$. However, in order to boost the oxygen concentration in the air supplied by the blower, the oxygen flow quantity may increase greatly. As a result, the rate of utilization of oxygen at the cathode will fall. As shown in Table 10, in System A, the capacity reduction effect of the fuel cell is fairly small by reducing the oxygen utilization rate when compared with System B. The reduction effect of the fuel cell capacity is so large that the difference between the load for the high load sampling time of $E_{d,t} > E_{set}$ of the load pattern of a building and the low load sampling time of $E_{d,t} < E_{set}$ is large. This typical case is a load pattern of the factory, and is common in System A and System B. The capacity reduction effect of the fuel cell is influenced by frequency of appearance of the high load and the low load. There is little appearance frequency of low loads, and when the values of the loads are large, the capacity reduction effect of the fuel cell is very small. The load pattern of the hotel is a typical example of this. Moreover, when changes in the load are small through one day, the reduction effect of the fuel cell capacity is small in both systems, and the load pattern of the small store is an example of this. When there are sufficient occasions to produce hydrogen and oxygen for reducing a load peak, the reduction method of the fuel cell capacity of using the water electrolysis system is effective. The time period of low loading and high load is divided clearly, and since the difference between low loading and the high load is large, the load pattern for the hospital and the factory is sufficient for the production of hydrogen and oxygen by water electrolysis. As a result, the power-generation capacity of the fuel cell is greatly reduced. In the case of the individual house, the capacity of the electric power is decided by the cooling load in summer. In an individual house, although the load fluctuation is large, before and after night or daytime, the load is small and a large amount of hydrogen and oxygen can be produced during these periods. By introducing System B into an individual house, the effect of capacity reduction of the fuel cell stack is large.

Town Gas Consumption

Figures 38 and 39 show the calculation results of the town gas consumption as a result of the introduction of System A and System B to each building, respectively. The calculated town gas consumption on representative days each month from the analysis results are shown in Figures 40 and 41. Figure 40 shows the town gas consumption for monthly representative days in the individual house, and Figure 41 shows the results of town gas consumption in other buildings. The conventional method in Figures 40 and 41 is an operational method which follows the power load, except for the water electrolysis equipment of the system shown in Figure 29. The efficiency η_{RM} of the reformer in the conventional method changes with the value of the load. The model showing the relationship between the power load of the fuel cell system with a reformer and the generation efficiency of this system is shown in Figure 42 [23, 24, 29, 30]. The town gas consumptions of the conventional method shown in Figures 40 and 41 are calculation results when carrying out load-following operation using the characteristic of Figure 42. In the calculation results for each monthly representative day of each load pattern for the individual house, the hospital, and the factory, the reduction effect of the town gas consumption in System B is larger than the conventional method. However, for May and August representative days for the hotel, and every monthly representative day for the small store, System A and System B cannot reduce the town gas consumption in the conventional method. This is because partial loads with low efficiency occur frequently which increases the town gas consumption, if the load following operation by the conventional method is introduced into each load pattern for the individual house, the hospital, and the factory. On the other hand, when introducing the conventional method into the load pattern of a hotel or a small store, a drop in the efficiency of the system has a small sampling time of a partial load with low efficiency few.

Reformer and Auxiliary Machines Operation

The reformer is stopped in the sampling time when there is no consumption of town gas in Figures 38 and 39. As shown in each figure, since the floating loads are small, the reformer can operate at a maximum efficiency point. Since starting and stopping of the reformer takes nearly 20 minutes, it is necessary to reduce the number of times this occurs which will also reduce consumption of energy [23, 24] . As shown in Figures 38 and 39 (a), (b), (c), in the load patterns of the individual house, the hospital, and the factory, the reformer can be stopped on many sampling time zones, respectively. Therefore, if the operational methods using System A or System B are introduced, starting and stopping will only occur once or twice each day.

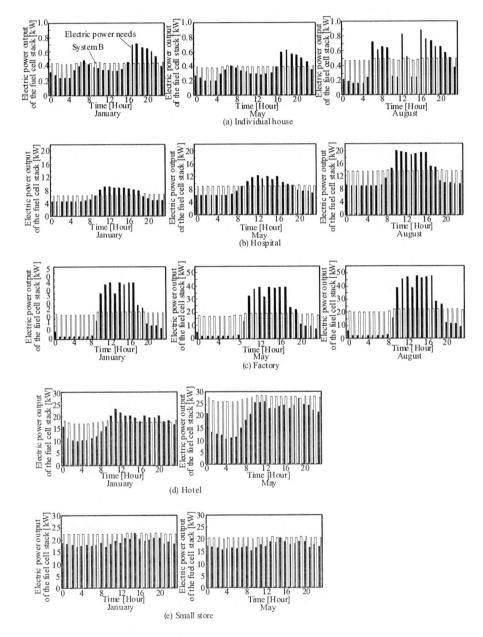

Figure 37. Operation planning of system B.

Table 10. Fuel cell capacity reduction effect

	Conventional method	System A	System B
(a) Individual house	0.94 kW	0.7 kW	0.49 kW
(b) Hospital	22.0 kW	18.2 kW	13.6 kW
(c) Factory	50.0 kW	36.0 kW	23.0 kW
(d) Hotel	41.0 kW, 28.0kW(May)	40.0 kW	(27.2 kW)
(e) Small store	24.0 kW(January)	(21.8 kW)	(21.8 kW)

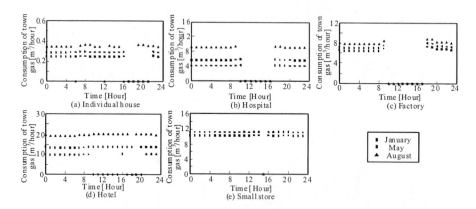

Figure 38. Town gas consumption using system A.

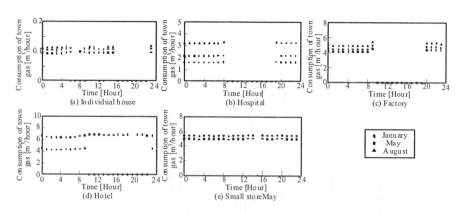

Figure 39. Town gas consumption of the sytem B.

On each monthly representative day for each building, the calculation results of the number of times required for the operation of blowers B_1, B_2 and B_3 are shown in Figure 43. There is more operational time required of the blowers for System A, except for the results of the small store, when compared to System B. The reasons for this include operation of the reformer at times of high load, mixing of the hydrogen from the gas cylinder with the reformed gas, and supplying the fuel cell.

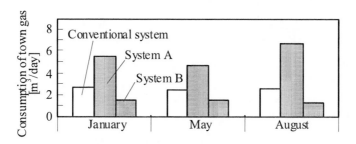

Figure 40. Town gas consumption of the representation day of the system A and the system B introduced into the individual house.

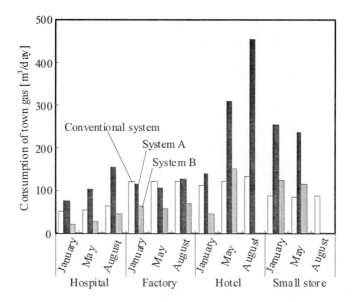

Figure 41. Town gas consumption of the representation day of the system A and the system B introduced into the individual house, factory, hotel, small store and office.

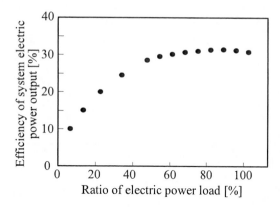

Figure 42. The related curve of the ratio of power load of a fuel cell system with reformer, and efficiency of electric power output.

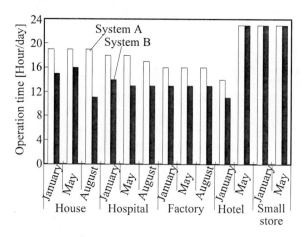

Figure 43. Operation time of the blower B_1, B_2, B_3.

CONCLUSION

If gas with a high oxygen concentration is supplied, rather than air, to the cathode of a fuel cell stack, the generation efficiency of the fuel cell improves. A reduction in the installed capacity of a fuel cell stack was attempted in this study using this power-generation characteristic.

During periods of small electricity demand, the fuel cell is operated with reformed gas and air, along with simultaneous water electrolysis operation. Hydrogen and oxygen are produced by water electrolysis, and compression storage of these gases is carried out in cylinders. On the other hand, when the electric power load is large, the cylinder gases are supplied to the fuel cell. In this case, the town gas consumption is smaller using the method which supplies hydrogen and oxygen of cylinders to the fuel cell directly for specific load patterns, such as the individual house, the hospital, and the factory, rather than mixing hydrogen and oxygen of the cylinders with the reformer and blower air.

In order to introduce a water electrolysis system and to obtain a larger reduction effect of the capacity of the fuel cell stack, sufficient hydrogen and oxygen to reduce the load peak must be produced. Therefore, the reduction effect of the fuel cell capacity changes with the load pattern. The periods of low and high loads are divided clearly, and the effect is large when the difference between the low load and high load values is large.

If the load-following operation of a building with load fluctuation is performed by a fuel cell system with a reformer, partial load operation with low efficiency will occur frequently. According to the operational method of the system proposed in this section, the load fluctuation range of a reformer is narrow and drops in efficiency can be prevented. Moreover, the number of times of starting and stopping of a reformer can be limited to once or twice each day.

INDEX